MW01201385

Justice
in
Everyday Life

Justice
in
Everyday Life

A Look at the Social Principles
of
The United Methodist Church

Neal Christie

DISCIPLESHIP RESOURCES

PO BOX 340003 • NASHVILLE, TN 37203-0003
www.discipleshipresources.org

ISBNs
Print: 978-0-88177-652-2
Epub: 978-0-88177-653-9
Mobi: 978-0-88177-654-6

Scripture quotations not otherwise identified are from the New Revised Standard Version Bible © 1989, Division of Christian Education of the National Council of the Churches of Christ in the United States of America. Used by permission. All rights reserved.

Scripture quotations noted *The Message* are from *THE MESSAGE*. Copyright © by Eugene H. Peterson 1993, 1994, 1995, 1996, 2000, 2001, 2002. Used by permission of NavPress Publishing Group.

Scripture quotations noted NIV are from The Holy Bible, New International Version® NIV® Copyright © 1973, 1978, 1984, 2011 by Biblica, Inc.™ Used by permission. All rights reserved worldwide.

The designation *UMH* refers to *The United Methodist Hymnal*. Copyright © 1989 by The United Methodist Publishing House.

The designation *TFWS* refers to *The Faith We Sing*. Copyright © 2000 by Abingdon.

JUSTICE IN EVERYDAY LIFE: A Look at the Social Principles of The United Methodist Church. Copyright © 2014 Discipleship Resources. All rights reserved. No part of this book may be reproduced in any form whatsoever, print or electronic, without written permission from the publisher, except in the case of brief quotations embodied in critical articles or reviews. For information regarding rights and permissions, contact Discipleship Resources, PO Box 340003, Nashville, TN 37203-0003.

Library of Congress Control Number: 2013950575

Printed in the United States of America

DR652

CONTENTS

PREFACE
TEACHING AND LEARNING

How we teach is as important as what we teach; how we learn is as important as what we learn. Adults respond to particular teaching and learning styles, and one person's style of learning may be similar to others in a group, or it may be different. This Lay Servant Ministries advanced course provides you with an opportunity to tailor learning and teaching to your own style. It also challenges you to craft your teaching and facilitation styles to meet the emerging needs of your students.

Changes within the life of a group invite you to modify your presentation style to meet unforeseen needs. Participants bring to sessions a wealth of lived experience, learned knowledge, and Christ-centered curiosity. Your goal is to support them as they speak from their hearts and minds: challenge their beliefs without shattering them, share from your personal life experience, and know when it is inappropriate to overshadow the beliefs or experiences of another person.

Your role is to create space for genuine dialogue to occur. Genuine dialogue seeks to hear from a participant's own perspectives and also includes the richly textured Christian tradition to which we belong. You are called to lead participants to confirm, question, clarify, and expand on how they practice the United Methodist tradition in light of the Social Principles of The United Methodist Church.

Flexibility and adaptability are essential practices for any teacher. As teachers and facilitators, our goal is to create a culture of learning with students, and to be creative and open to the Spirit's leanings.

Remember: Teaching or facilitation styles may be auditory, visual, or tactile.

Here are several examples:

Auditory

- Open class discussion
- Show-and-tell
- Debate
- Paraphrase
- Music
- Songs or rhymes
- Poetry
- Storytelling
- Reading/writing/journaling
- Word games
- Lecture

Visual

- Illustrations and pictures
- Charts and graphs
- Time lines
- Diagrams
- Cartoons
- Bulletin boards
- Photographs
- Magazines and newspapers
- Videos
- Posters
- Montages and collages
- Collections of crafts

Tactile

- Games
- Simulations
- Painting
- Puppets
- Sculpting
- Drama
- Dance
- Signing
- Construction
- Experiments
- Role-playing
- Origami
- Jigsaw puzzles

A WORD OF WELCOME TO STUDENTS FROM THE INSTRUCTOR

The following welcome may be given during the first session or sent to students in a letter when they enroll in the class. The goal is to prepare persons to actively participate with open minds, assured that their own experiences and opinions will be valued:

Welcome to this advanced course in Lay Servant Ministries. Lay servants commit to preparing themselves for each session. Through study and prayer, they will ensure that they are ready to use their skills to support and encourage others in learning.

Some of the steps associated with serving as a lay servant do not always come easily or bear immediate fruit. Be patient. Part of your responsibility as servant leaders is to model persistence.

The most important part of your preparation for this course is to pay attention to your own soul and spiritual life. You can do this by practicing the classic spiritual disciplines of the Christian faith, shaped by our Wesleyan tradition. These practices include:

- prayers of confession, lament, intercession, gratitude, and praise
- small-group welcome and accountability
- Bible study and rigorous reflection on scripture read in context
- creating community among persons who are poor and marginalized
- offering hospitality to persons who suffer and are in need
- corporate worship

- tithing and extravagant generosity
- frequent celebration of the Eucharist in communion with others
- fasting and simplified living
- Christian conferencing
- practicing sabbath time apart and listening for God in silence
- advocating for sustained public acts of mercy and justice
- mentoring and befriending others as they grow in their faith

Lay servants initiate and participate in ministries of caring and justice, lead mission trips, chair church committees, teach Sunday school classes, and host midweek study groups—all in a greater effort to expand the church's witness and inspire others to a deeper commitment to Christ and a more faithful life of discipleship.

Lay servants appreciate the Wesleyan approach to faith revealed in scripture, illuminated by tradition, brought alive in personal and communal experience, and confirmed by rigorous reasoning. Lay servants help participants describe what is happening in the church and world and imagine what is possible through the life, death, and resurrection of Jesus Christ.

Before your first session you are encouraged to:

- come prepared to learn from and with other participants.
- pray for your instructor as well as others in the course.

In the process of learning and responding to new insights and knowledge, trust that you and your peers will receive an abundance of grace and peace through our Lord Jesus Christ.

Practice good dialogue with your peers and be open to how United Methodists can live as advocates in church and society on behalf of Christ.

Consider your session's goals and outcomes. Each session is designed to enhance your desire for deeper learning that leads to more committed Christian action modeled after the life of Jesus.

Thank you for your leadership and participation in this course.

INTRODUCTION TO THE
SOCIAL PRINCIPLES

The Social Principles of The United Methodist Church are a call to a "prayerful, studied dialogue of faith and practice." They are statements of belief and practice spoken both to the church and to society.

The Social Principles are a product of prayer, but they also lead us to fervent prayer. The Social Principles begin with holy conferencing by people of faith, but they must be practiced to have any real value. The Social Principles emerge from the will of the church, but they reflect the needs of society as well as the church.

Some lifelong United Methodists become defensive when a new idea seems to conflict with a principle they hold. Other United Methodists are overjoyed that what their consciences and experiences have taught them is in accord with the Social Principles. As you read the Social Principles, you may find yourself nodding in agreement at times to some principles and responding negatively to others.

Remember, General Conference is held every four years. It is the only entity to speak officially for the denomination through *The Book of Discipline* and *The Book of Resolutions*. Each of the more than forty thousand local churches in more than one hundred conferences in Africa, the Philippines, Europe, and the United States elects approximately one thousand delegates to General Conference. Half are laypersons and the other half are clergy. These delegates determine the Social Principles, mandates, and resolutions of The United Methodist Church.

Any United Methodist person, local church, conference, agency, caucus, or group may propose changes to the Social Principles at General Conference. Petitions are written and submitted in advance of the quadrennial meeting. Once at General Conference, delegates discuss and vote on petitions. If supported, the petitions are included in either *The Book of Discipline* or *The Book of Resolutions*.

The Social Principles, though not church law, are part of the *Discipline*. They are intended to be "instructive and persuasive in the best of the prophetic spirit," according to their preface. "They are a prayerful and thoughtful effort on the part of the General Conference to speak to the human issues in the contemporary world from a sound biblical and theological foundation."

Do you remember the last time you were persuaded by someone? What caused you to change your mind or choose to do something differently? Encourage your students to consider this about themselves.

What images come to mind when you hear the word *prophet*? What do you least like about the prophets in the Bible and what do you find most appealing about them?

In what ways does the Bible's message of salvation, written to entire communities, call us as individuals to pursue, in the words of John Wesley, "social holiness"?

Invite your students to relax and enter into a "prayerful, studied dialogue" with themselves, with God, and with others as they look at matters of faith and practice. Encourage them to remain open to the Holy Spirit.

What Difference Do the Social Principles Make for the Church?

The Social Principles embody another way to understand the role of the church as it speaks and acts upon its convictions in the public sphere. The Social Principles are The United Methodist Church's attempt to accomplish three important tasks:

- **Speak prophetically.** What shall the church say and what shall the church do to transform the world into the beloved community—the kingdom of God—imagined by Jesus and taught by his disciples?

  Remember, while the prophets did not attempt to predict the future, they were passionate about trying to change it. They sought to address social problems and resolve social tension. Their faith was public and personal but never private.

  The Social Principles are prophetic statements intended for both the church and society. Change or transformation must happen through an inward as well as an outward spiritual journey. Social transformation to create a more hospitable, just, and Christlike world demonstrates a deeper conversion than a single decision to follow Christ.

When the Social Principles speak prophetically, they do not polarize people based on adherence to a particular position. Rather, they name problems and pose possible solutions appropriate to the context in which we live.

- **Respond biblically.** When biblical faith is spoken prophetically, persons are challenged in deep, abiding love to realign their personal habits, behaviors, and attitudes more closely with the will of God. In Jesus Christ, the Almighty came to deliver, liberate, and restore persons and communities to live in a way that exhibits the restoration of God's image in the world.

  Social holiness is always evangelical; it is always invitational. Social holiness compels us to expand our reach of humility, mercy, compassion, justice, and reconciliation in the spirit of Jesus. Social holiness requires us to speak our convictions and stand by them in the public square.

- **Act pastorally.** How shall the church respond to people's hurts, pains, and struggles? How does the plight of the world's needs wound our souls? We have a responsibility to care for one another, especially the vulnerable among us, with mutual concern and love.

  The Social Principles identify personal and social crises and offer a pastoral response. In this sense, the Social Principles are understood less as legalistic public statements and more as therapeutic in purpose. They go well beyond pragmatic problem solving. They direct us to prioritize the restoration and mending of our relationships with God, nature, our neighbors, our enemies, and with ourselves.

What All of the Social Principles Have in Common

Each Social Principle is actually a number of things:

- **A position.** The United Methodist Church takes a public stand on many timely issues. While we may not all agree with these positions, a public stand is a plumb line or common starting point for dialogue. The Social Principles are a barometer to determine how close we as a church and society measure up to God's vision for right relationships with one another and our neighbors.

  It has been said, "If you can't stand for something, you'll fall for anything." Where do you stand? What are you still undecided about? How did you reach the convictions you presently hold? Have you ever changed those convictions?

- **A set of interests.** To one degree or another, we all act out of our self-interests. As human beings we have multiple self-interests that compete for our attention and even our undivided allegiance. The Latin term for interest actually means "inter" and "esse" or "to be among."

  Interests are determined by those we live among. Our interests may be the result of our access to work and education, our ethnicities and racial identities, our nationalities, genders, ages, or political affiliations. Whose interests do the Social Principles reflect? Whose interests appear to be missing from the Social Principles?

  The positions set forth in the Social Principles are an effort to mediate potentially conflicting interests that arise from diverse and perhaps divergent groups in church and society. These positions point to issues where we must practice respect and tolerance.

- **A set of core values.** Every culture communicates and passes down a set of traditions or values from one generation to the next. We reflect to a greater or lesser degree the cultures we inhabit. Our values may either complement or contradict the cultural expectations of other people of good faith. What do you value? How and where did you learn what to value?

  As Christians we are meant to move beyond our own cultural expectations. Biblical values ought to shape who we are in the world. We are no longer slaves to cultural practices that contradict the gospel of Jesus Christ. At the same time, we bring with us the texture and the tenor of our cultures to enliven our understanding of who Jesus is for us today.

  What are some biblical values that we hold in common? What do you identify as values unique to The United Methodist Church?

- **Response to human need.** When we cannot agree with the public positions our denomination takes, our self-interests are at odds, and our values seem to be incompatible, can we not still agree on some basic human needs that must be met for all to retain their humanity?

  What basic needs do we all hold in common? Needs such as food, shelter, work, safety, community, and faith are addressed in the Social Principles. Specific prescriptions are offered in the Social Principles that point to what it will take to meet those needs.

A Word to the Course Leader

Course leaders convey ideas and information. They model course content by how they teach, lead, and relate to group members. The practices and behaviors that make for good course leaders are highlighted below.

- Partnership. In working with the Lay Servant Committee—your model of information—experiences and context for learning are the foundations for partnership. Learning happens as everyone interacts and actively constructs new knowledge through dialogue and shared experiences.
- Hospitality. Create a hospitable environment for your students so they feel welcomed and included. Ensure that the meeting room is a comfortable temperature, has adequate space, is furnished with comfortable chairs, and has good lighting. Arrange the room so everyone can see both you and your flip chart. Place the chairs in a circle or "U" shape to facilitate conversation.

  Try to create an environment where participants understand and draw from shared experiences.
- Model Listening. Encourage students to listen carefully to one another. When persons feel they are heard, they are generally more willing to speak. Adult learners actively construct new knowledge and behavior through discussion. Model deep listening to send a powerful message about its importance as a discipline for learning and transformation.
- Model Practicing the Means of Grace. We all share one overarching purpose: to form disciples of Jesus Christ who can apply their faith to everyday choices in a diverse, disorienting world.

Basic Resources Needed for the Course

- The Bible (at least one version should be the New Revised Standard Version [NRSV])
- *The Book of Discipline*, current edition
- *The Book of Resolutions*, current edition
- *Social Principles of The United Methodist Church*, current edition
- *The United Methodist Hymnal*
- *The Faith We Sing*
- A blank journal

Each student should have a copy of the most recent edition of the *Social Principles of The United Methodist Church* and a journal. You can either include it in the course materials if your registration fee is adequate to do so, or require students to purchase a copy before they begin the course. Be sure *The Book of Discipline* and *The Book of Resolutions* are available for review and reference. Participants should bring their Bibles to each session.

Both you and your fellow learners bring a wealth of experience and knowledge to the learning encounter. Help one another name these experiences; use them as a springboard to new learning.

Additional Materials (needed for some or all of the sessions)

- Index cards or adhesive notes
- Pencils/pens
- Markers
- Flip chart, dry-erase board, or chalkboard
- Tape
- Pictures of people, technology, religion, nature, or other images that may reflect issues raised in the Social Principles and Social Creed
- Newspapers/magazines (recent)
- Globe and/or world map
- Potted plant
- Candle
- Matches
- Chocolate candy bar

- Cotton shirt
- Plastic tire or plastic cup
- Glass filled with water
- Sand
- Large open space where the group can easily move around

Preparation

This course is divided into five two-hour sessions. You may wish to complete this study through ten one-hour sessions or four Saturday sessions of two and one-half hours each. Each session builds on the previous; reviewing content before and after each session will help maintain continuity. If you choose to combine sessions, you may eliminate the closing and opening worship between sessions.

Before each session, review the section of the *Social Principles of The United Methodist Church* booklet that will be covered; be sure to assemble necessary materials.

Session One

Part One: Introduction to the Course

Learning Goals

- To understand that questioning the Social Principles and having a positive critical attitude toward the *Discipline* and your faith is not a hindrance, but a necessity if the Social Principles are to be grasped and put into practice
- To examine the Social Principles and their relationship to the Bible and to study their roots in the Wesleyan tradition expressed through The United Methodist Church
- To understand the development of the Social Principles throughout the great drama of spiritually motivated movements for social change that has occurred over thousands of years

Preparation

Read the booklet *Social Principles of The United Methodist Church* (make sure you have the current edition). Keep the chair next to you vacant as a visible sign of welcome for the unseen guest. Remind participants that the circle is never complete and that the Holy Spirit has a way of interrupting our well-laid plans and agendas.

We are intentional in reserving space for God to come and join the circle. We invite God into the circle. We recognize that God is within the circle, preparing the way.

Prepare six index cards or adhesive notes with the six major rubrics of the Social Principles written on them: Natural World, Nurturing Community, Social Community, Economic Community, Political Community, and World Community.

Display the cards/notes for the class. Have additional index cards or adhesive notes and pencils or pens for participants. Cut out pictures of people, technology, religion, nature, or anything that may reflect issues in the Social Principles from magazines and newspapers. If time permits, laminate the pictures before the first session.

If you plan to use the alternate worship for this session (see appendix), bring to the class a globe, world map, potted plant, candle, matches or lighter, a chocolate candy bar, a cotton shirt, a plastic tire or plastic cup, and a glass filled with water.

Session Plan

Welcome and Introductions (15 Minutes). Ask the class to form pairs. Explain that each person will introduce his or her partner to the larger group. Choose one of the following models for this exercise:

1. Learn your partner's name and ask him or her to share some unique personal information and why he or she joined the class. Allow for a pause in the conversation between speakers so that all voices can be heard.
2. Read John 1:1-5, 14. In *The Message* verse 14 reads in part, "The Word became flesh and blood, and moved into the neighborhood." Ask your partner to describe her or his neighborhood: Who lives there? How is God in Christ present there? What impact does the church have on society in "the neighborhood," and what influence does society have on both the local church and the global church?

Allow each pair approximately three minutes of discussion. Then have each pair present their findings to the class.

General Information (5 Minutes). Inform the class of the locations of restrooms, the resource table, and any other information participants may need to know.

Opening Worship (10 Minutes). Explain to the class that worship expresses and forms Christian community. As we turn to worship, we have already begun to form a community that can express God's praise, glory, and intention for justice and care for all people. Tell the class that the empty chair beside you will represent the presence of Christ in each session.

Review (20 Minutes). Review all of the information from the "Welcome" through "Worship" sections so that everyone understands what this session will accomplish. In your own words, present the "Introduction to the Social Principles" found on pages 11–15. Invite volunteers to read this section aloud a few paragraphs at a time. If time will not permit you to read the entire section, finish reading it at the beginning of the next session.

Activity (20 Minutes). Explain to participants that each picture you have gathered from magazines or newspapers is an icon. The pictures present real-life situations. They describe the world around us, and they show how we interpret the world to others.

The church is called to be principled, but not ideological. The church is not aligned with political parties. The church does not take partisan positions. The church does, however, make ethically informed, theologically cogent public statements about problems in society.

The church is called to be clear, but also civil. The United Methodist Church advocates for mercy and justice, and strives not to become self-righteous in the process. We know that the church itself is not exempt from social critique, so we apply the Social Principles to the way the church orders itself, the values it communicates, and the needs it addresses.

The church is called to be engaged, but not to be used. The church of Jesus Christ is engaged in dialogue with the institutions of society. These may include local social service and civic groups, nongovernmental offices, nonprofit agencies, and national political groups, including parliaments and congresses and the United Nations. In each encounter the church affirms its own vision for the way the world ought to be as seen through the eyes of God. The Social Principles invite us to make a different world, not just a difference in this world.

1. Ask participants to select one of the images from those you gathered before the session. Ask them to journal on one of these questions:

   When I reflect on this image I feel . . .
   It reminds me of . . .
   It moves me to do or change . . .

2. Ask participants to write on an adhesive note or index card the title of a social justice concern the image brings to mind. Ask everyone to give his or her image a title. Ask each

participant to post his or her image and title on the adhesive note or index card in the Social Principles category in which he or she thinks it would be found.

3. Invite participants to discuss what their images and titles have in common and where they are distinct.

4. Ask the class to discuss what principles the images convey. Are they positive, negative, or neutral principles?

5. Ask the class in what ways the church is called to apply these principles based on what they see in the images.

6. Again, based on the images, how does the church stand apart from the world and present a new reality ushered in through Jesus Christ?

Break (5 Minutes). Allow a short break to shift gears and prepare to dig more deeply into the content.

Part Two: The Natural World

The remainder of this session will focus on "The Natural World" section in the *Social Principles* booklet. The goals of the second half of the session are:

- to understand more about God's creation
- to know that God has granted us stewardship of creation
- to act upon the natural world with loving care and respect
- to support an ecologically sustainable world with a higher quality of life

Spiritual Disciplines (25 Minutes). Invite the class to form six groups. Assign each group one of the sections from the Social Principles listed below (¶160). Ask the groups to read and then discuss the sections they have been assigned:

Group 1 — (¶160.A) Water, Air, Soil, Minerals, Plants
Group 2 — (¶160.B) Energy Resources Utilization
Group 3 — (¶160.C) Animal Life
Group 4 — (¶160.D) Global Climate Stewardship
Group 5 — (¶160.E) Space
Group 6 — (¶160.F) Science and Technology

Ask the class to discuss any theological concerns they have with the material. Invite them to consider the following questions about the section their group was assigned:

- Do I agree with the principle? Is my *position* based on a belief that I have learned? If so, where did I learn it? On what experiences do I base my position?
- Are any of the concerns I have about the Social Principles based on *interests* or those groups with which I am affiliated or connected that influence my beliefs and actions? Are my interests based on particular *values* that I affirm?
- Are the positions I take, the values I hold, and the interests I represent influenced by the Social Principles? How do my *positions, values, and interests influence my understanding of the needs* that our church and society seek to meet? In what ways are my responses based on the Wesleyan focus on scripture, tradition, experience, and reason?
- What beliefs do I hold about God that might help me decide what I as a Christian should think and do about these topics? What two major beliefs are stated about God in the introductory paragraph of the section on the natural world?

Make two lists of the various issues the Social Principles support in order to uphold and care for the natural world. Ask yourself: *Do I agree or disagree with each of the lists?*

Reconvene the Class. Ask each group to report on their discussions about the material covered. Allow time for any final comments or questions.

Discuss the First Paragraph of ¶160.I: "The Natural World" (10 Minutes). Display the following: a chocolate candy bar, a cotton shirt, a plastic tire or plastic cup, and a glass filled with water.

- Ask the class to brainstorm what these everyday objects have in common.
- Ask the class to list all the elements of God's creation that must come together to create these commodities. List all the various nations that contributed to creating these items.
- How did these become commodities? How do we determine the common value of these commodities today? Is their value based on their goodness as gifts of God or is it derived from their perceived use/value to human beings?
- What biblical images are evoked by the Natural World section of the Social Principles?

If time permits, make reference to the Council of Bishops' pastoral letter, "God's Renewed Creation," and its emphasis on the proliferation of weapons, abject poverty, and threats to the environment.

Session Review and Assignments (5 Minutes). Ask for volunteers to lead the opening worship for the next session. Ask participants to read the sections titled "The Nurturing Community" and "The Social Community" in the *Social Principles* booklet.

Closing Prayer (5 Minutes). There's an opportune time to do things, a right time for everything on the earth:

> A right time for birth and another for death,
> A right time to plant and another to reap,
> A right time to kill and another to heal,
> A right time to destroy and another to construct,
> A right time to cry and another to laugh,
> A right time to lament and another to cheer,
> A right time to make love and another to abstain,
> A right time to embrace and another to part,
> A right time to search and another to count your losses,
> A right time to hold on and another to let go,
> A right time to rip out and another to mend,
> A right time to shut up and another to speak up,
> A right time to love and another to hate,
> A right time to wage war and another to make peace.[1]

Assignments

- **In preparation for the next session:** Read at least three of the following scripture passages:

      Deuteronomy 17:14-20
      Deuteronomy 26:4-15
      Psalm 104:14-24
      Jeremiah 8:18-22
      Mark 10:2-12

Luke 19:45-47
Acts 4:32-37
Romans 12:14-21
James 2:1-7

1. Read the assigned scripture passage alone and then as a group.
2. What title would you give this passage of scripture?
3. What principle is communicated in the passage and whose interests are communicated? What value? What need?

All participants and leaders should also read the sections titled "The Nurturing Community" and "The Social Community" in the *Social Principles* booklet.

Part One: The Nurturing Community

Learning Goals

- To develop a better understanding of community
- To gain knowledge of the gospel of God's love for all
- To help maintain and strengthen the human community
- To practice respectful dialogue with all persons
- To determine the esteem that society holds for persons or groups
- To understand how we can safeguard human rights
- To respond in faith to acts of hate and violence against humankind

Preparation

You will need index cards, markers, tape, pens, recent newspapers, and recent newsmagazines.

Session Plan

Opening Worship (10 Minutes). Read the following quote aloud and reflect on it with the class:

> Our "Home" is the realm of God. It is where love and justice prevail, and we are
> called by God to make wherever we are as much like home as possible. We dare
> not feel "at home" in a world like this: where one-third of the people live abun-
> dantly, and two-thirds live in scarcity. . . . Christ breaks down the dividing wall.

"Home" happens when the walls come down, and the ghettos are no more, and we are all brothers and sisters. . . . Our footsteps down the aisle to share with others are the first short steps of the long journey "home."

—Richard Wilcox, "Spain"[2]

Ask for intercessory prayer concerns; then pray no. 570 in *The United Methodist Hymnal* together. Follow with the "Canticle of Love" (*UMH*, no. 646) or another hymn. Read Job 16:1-10 aloud; or, read or sing the words to "We Are Called" (*TFWS*, no. 2172); "They'll Know We Are Christians by Our Love" (*TFWS*, no. 2223); or "Gather Us In" (*TFWS*, no. 2236).

Allow time for a few moments of silence.

Review (5 Minutes). Ask participants if they have questions from the previous session.

Read and Discuss the First Paragraph of ¶161.II in the *Social Principles* Booklet (10 Minutes). Ask participants to journal on their first thoughts when they hear the word *community*. What words or thoughts initially come to mind when they hear the word *home*? Have participants share their journaling in pairs, noting similarities and dissimilarities.

Invite participants to reflect on the word *covenant*. You may want to write both *covenant* and *community* beside each other on a flip chart, dry-erase board, or chalkboard.

What beliefs, emotions, needs, and values do participants associate with the words *community* and *home*? What beliefs, emotions, needs, and values do these two words share?

What do the Social Principles describe as harmful to building community? What do they suggest is beneficial to building a community of integrity and health?

Based on participants' own experiences and what they have discussed so far, which Social Principles should take priority for the church and society today?

Optional Exercise. Ask for three volunteers. Using a marker and index card, "label" these volunteers with the following phrases:

1. Contemplated suicide
2. Survived family abuse
3. Chose to have an abortion

Distribute a pen and three index cards to each participant. Ask them to write on the index card the first word or phrase that comes to mind when they read each label (one response per situation per card). Ask participants to come forward and give their cards to each labeled volunteer. Then have a participant read each of the cards aloud.

After all the responses have been read, ask each volunteer, "How do these words make you feel?" Then ask the group, "What do these labels do to a person who wears them in church and society? What are the values these words convey, and what are the needs they represent? How do we nurture persons affected by these concerns?"

Invite the volunteers to remove their labels, and conclude the activity with prayer.

Spiritual Disciplines (30 Minutes). As the instructor leads the group, members should discuss the following questions. The instructor may want to divide these questions up so that participants discuss them in pairs or in groups of three:

- Why do you take your stance?
- How has the church changed its stance over time and why?
- What do you imagine The United Methodist Church will look like in fifty years?
- How might the church change its stance five hundred years into the future?

Invite the class to form six groups. Assign each group one of the sections from the Social Principles listed below (¶161). Ask the groups to read and then discuss the sections they have been assigned:

Group 1 — (¶161.A) The Family; (¶161.B) Marriage; (¶161.C) Divorce
Group 2 — (¶161.D) Single Persons; (¶161.E) Women and Men
Group 3 — (¶161.F) Human Sexuality; (¶161.G) Family Violence and Abuse
Group 4 — (¶161.H) Sexual Abuse; (¶161.I) Sexual Harassment
Group 5 — (¶161.J) Abortion; (¶161.K) Ministry to Those Who Have Experienced an Abortion; (¶161.L) Adoption
Group 6 — (¶161.M) Faithful Care for Dying Persons; (¶161.N) Suicide

Read aloud "Marks of a True Methodist" from *The Works of John Wesley*. In 1742, John Wesley delineated the aspects of practical divinity:

> The distinguishing marks of a Methodist are not his opinions of any sort. . . .
> While he thus always exercises his love to God, by praying without ceasing,
> rejoicing evermore, and in everything giving thanks, this commandment is

written in his heart, "That he who loveth God, love his brother also." And he accordingly loves his neighbor as himself; he loves every man as his own soul. His heart is full of love to all mankind, to every child of "the Father of the spirits of all flesh." That a man is not personally known to him, is no bar to his love; no, nor that he is known to be such as he approves not, that he repays hatred for his good-will. For he "loves his enemies"; yea, and the enemies of God, "the evil and the unthankful." And if it be not in his power to "do good to them that hate him," yet he ceases not to pray for them, though they continue to spurn his love, and still "despitefully use him and persecute him."[3]

John Wesley, the founder of the Methodist movement, affirmed that Methodists are known not as much for their particular beliefs as for their demonstrable actions, even toward those who disagree with them. Methodists care about virtuous character formation as well as testing such Christian character in real situations within the community. Hospitality in its most basic form is to practice how to be in right relationship with others. When early Methodists were an emerging and still minority community, Wesley's advice perhaps carried a different meaning than when the Methodist organization became a mainline religious tradition alongside other Christian denominations.

Wesley was adamant: We simply cannot claim the marks of a Methodist in social isolation, disengaged from the troubles of the world. Holy consternation cajoles us into taking up the causes of the outcasts—those whose backs are up against the wall—and to act with equity and justice toward others in society.

Each of the Social Principles in this section responds to the urgency to instill and sustain the qualities of the beloved and just community in our congregations.

Ask participants to form small groups of two or three and discuss the following questions:

- Do the Nurturing Community sections of the Social Principles reflect Wesley's marks of a Methodist? If so, in what way?
- What happens when persons are deprived of community and do not develop their capacity to practice the marks of Methodism? Can you name some examples?

Invite the Class to Reconvene. Ask each group to speak about its own illustrations and examples of problems addressed in the Social Principles read for today's class.

Break (5 Minutes). Allow a short break to shift gears and prepare to dig more deeply into the content.

Part Two: The Social Community

Read and Discuss the Bible (15 Minutes). Read Matthew 11:2-6 aloud. Invite participants to think about why John asked the question in verse 3, and to then think about Jesus' response to John.

You may wish to point out that at the end of this conversation, Jesus' response might be summarized by these words: Look for deeds, not theological essays.

Invite participants to write or draw in their journals a response to this biblical text as it relates to the social community.

Discuss Rights and Responsibilities. Distribute newspapers and newsmagazines. Ask one-half of the group to brainstorm definitions for *responsibility* and the other half to brainstorm definitions for *rights*. Ask each group to find recent stories in the newspapers and magazines that illustrate their understandings of rights and responsibilities.

Allow participants enough time to work out their definitions, and ask the groups to share their definitions with the entire class.

Ask the class to identify what rights and responsibilities they have in common as well as the ways they differ. What would you include in the categories of rights and responsibilities that may not be named in the Social Principles? Are rights and responsibilities culturally bound or do they cross regions and national borders?

Ask participants the following question: Where do the Social Principles, in the Social Community section, speak clearly about human *rights* and human *responsibilities*?

Draw a picture of a human being on a flip chart, dry-erase board, or chalkboard. Ask the class the following questions:

- Why did our Creator put legs on us? (For freedom of movement.)
- Why did the Creator put mouths on us? (For freedom of speech.)
- Hands? (For the right to work.)

Continue this exercise until you have accounted for many of the observable attributes that make up a human being: a heart for a soul and freedom of religion, a stomach for the intake of food, and so on.

Human dignity and other human rights are not assigned to us by a government. They are given to us as gifts from God. When we take a few minutes to observe the form and shape our human bodies share and the various functions our bodies perform every day, we are reminded that regardless of our political leanings or the form of government our society chooses to take, we are all made in the image of our Creator and given particular rights and responsibilities to exercise in society.

Explore ¶162.III (35 Minutes). Read the opening paragraph of the Social Community section from *The Book of Discipline* aloud as an overview to the small-group exercise below.

Invite the class to form nine groups. Assign each group one of the sections from the Social Principles listed below (¶162). Ask the groups to read and then discuss the sections they have been assigned.

Group 1 — (¶162.A) Rights of Racial and Ethnic Persons; (¶162.B) Rights of Religious Minorities

Group 2 — (¶162.C) Rights of Children; (¶162.D) Rights of Young People

Group 3 — (¶162.E) Rights of the Aging; (¶162.F) Rights of Women; (¶162.G) Rights of Men

Group 4 — (¶162.H) Rights of Immigrants; (¶162.I) Rights of Persons with Disabilities

Group 5 — (¶162.J) Equal Rights Regardless of Sexual Orientation; (¶162.K) Population

Group 6 — (¶162.L) Alcohol and Other Drugs; (¶162.M) Tobacco; (¶162.N) Medical Experimentation; (¶162.O) Genetic Technology

Group 7 — (¶162.P) Rural Life; (¶162.Q) Sustainable Agriculture; (¶162.R) Urban-Suburban Life

Group 8 — (¶162.S) Media Violence and Christian Values; (¶162.T) Information Communication Technology

Group 9 — (¶162.U) Persons Living with HIV and AIDS; (¶162.V) Right to Health Care; (¶162.W) Organ Transplantation and Donation

After approximately twenty minutes, ask each small group to report its summary statements to the entire class.

Ask the class the following questions:

• Which statement surprised you in a positive way?

- Which statement surprised you in a negative way?
- Which statement connects with the life of your church and your community? How?
- Which statement seems the most controversial to you and for the church today? Why?

Session Review and Assignments (5 Minutes). Ask for volunteers to lead the opening worship for the next session. Ask participants to notice during the week how many rights they exercise as a result of their place in society. Ask participants to list all the responsibilities they have as members of society and as United Methodist Christians and to bring the list to the following session.

Ask participants to read the Economic Community section in the *Social Principles* booklet and note any questions that arise.

Closing Prayer (5 Minutes)

> Dear God, thank you for all that is good, for our creation and for our humanity, for the stewardship you have given us of this planet earth, for the gifts of life and of one another, for your love, which is unbounded and eternal. O thou, most holy and beloved, my Companion, my Guide upon the way, my bright evening star. We repent the wrongs we have done.

> —"Night Prayer," *A New Zealand Prayer Book*[4]

Part One: Teaching the Social Principles

Learning Goals

- To practice experiential group exercises to better inform understanding of the Social Principles
- To use creativity as a tool to discover deeper learning
- To communicate the Social Principles to diverse audiences
- To understand that all economic systems are under the judgment of God
- To discover that we have both public and private responsibilities toward the have-nots in our society
- To discern how our economic choices affect other people

Preparation

Bring your copy of the *Social Principles* to this session.

Session Plan

Opening Worship (10 Minutes). Ask for prayer concerns from the group and offer a prayer such as "For True Singing" (*UMH*, no. 69). Read or sing together "When in Our Music God Is Glorified" (*UMH*, no. 68); "Make Me a Channel of Your Peace" (*TFWS*, no. 2171); or "Joy in the Morning" (*TFWS*, no. 2284). Read Hebrews 13:1-8 aloud.

Review (5 Minutes). Ask the participants if they have any questions from the previous session.

Spiritual Disciplines I—Agree/Disagree (20 Minutes). Instruct the class to turn to the section titled "Teaching the Social Principles" in their *Social Principles of The United Methodist Church* booklets. Read the first two paragraphs under "Agree/Disagree" aloud. If your group needs a primer in United Methodist polity, you can read that section as well.

Read a statement from the material that has already been covered in the course (¶¶160–162). Ask participants to stand in one area of the learning space if they agree with the statement and another area if they disagree with it. Persons who have reservations, cannot make up their minds, or wish to remain neutral may stay in the middle of the room.

Once everyone has decided in which place to stand, invite two or three persons from each group to explain the position of their group and to articulate a biblical and theological basis for it. Repeat this exercise with different statements from the *Social Principles* as time permits.

Spiritual Disciplines II—Cross the Line/Raise Your Card (15 Minutes). Turn to the page in the *Social Principles of The United Methodist Church* booklet that discusses the "Cross the Line/Raise Your Card" exercise. Read or summarize the instructions. Form two lines of people about ten feet apart. The lines should face each other. Instruct participants to stand shoulder to shoulder in their line. Ask the questions from the list in the *Social Principles* booklet. You may ask several people to offer the reasons for their answers. This exercise will allow participants to think through their responses without debating or arguing with one another.

Reflection (10 Minutes). Ask the class to form two groups and read one of the following scripture passages:

- Group A: Luke 6:39-42
- Group B: Romans 5:18–6:4

Ask participants to paraphrase each scripture passage in their own words and discuss how it relates to the Nurturing Community section.

In light of these two scripture passages and the responses from the Agree/Disagree exercise, ask participants to discuss which statements they would rewrite and why. Ask the class two or more of the following questions:

1. What images and feelings did this exercise provoke?

2. What surprised you about your own or another's response?

3. How did it feel to stand alone or to stand with others?

4. Did you learn anything about someone in the class?

5. How do your position and experience on an issue inform the stated position?

6. What questions would you have liked to have heard asked? Why?

Break (5 Minutes). Allow a short break to shift gears and prepare to dig more deeply into the content.

Part Two: The Economic Community

Introduce the Concept of Economy (5 Minutes). Tell the class that the term *economy* comes from the Greek *oikos*, which means "household." Interestingly, it is also the root of two words in the English language: *ecology* and *economics*. Although these words do not seem to go together, it makes sense because ecology is the interactions in natural communities, and economics is the use of resources within this community. If we put these together, it reminds us how connected resources and interactions are within the church and the world as a whole.

When we look at the word *economy* as it applies to our daily lives, we are reminded to pray. Pray for the household of God—the church—as it seeks to be a responsible caretaker and advocate for the poor and the marginalized.

Read Deuteronomy 26. Here the Israelites are instructed in the way to order their lives and society after the Exodus from Egypt. Now that they have come through the wilderness and have reached the Promised Land, they must perform three acts:

1. Freed slaves are to give to God the firstfruits of the land with which they have been blessed.

2. They are to tell and retell the story of their deliverance so that they and their descendants are forever mindful of their utter reliance and dependence on God as their deliverer and sustainer.

3. They are to keep their covenant with God not out of fear, but out of a sincere desire to love their neighbors.

Invite participants to consider how retelling the story of the Exodus connects them with the specific priorities named in the Economic Community section of the Social Principles.

Explore the Economic Community (15 Minutes). Invite the class to form five groups. Assign each group one of the sections from the Social Principles listed below (¶163). Ask the groups to read and then discuss the sections they have been assigned.

Group 1 — (¶163.A) Property; (¶163.B) Collective Bargaining
Group 2 — (¶163.C) Work and Leisure; (¶163.D) Consumption
Group 3 — (¶163.E) Poverty; (¶163.F) Foreign Workers
Group 4 — (¶163.G) Gambling; (¶163.H) Family Farms
Group 5 — (¶163.I) Corporate Responsibility; (¶163.J) Finance

Ask each group to summarize in their own words the sections they were assigned. Ask participants if they were surprised by these topics and whether they think that the church is overstepping its responsibility or its right to speak about these topics.

Explore the Bible (25 Minutes). Invite participants to form groups of two or three persons. Assign each group one of the scripture passages listed below. Ask each group to identify any economic change that occurs in the passage. Invite the groups to reflect on the connections between economic justice, political justice, and community.

- Exodus 1:8-14; 2:23-25; 3:7-10: Taking God's Side (Changing Sides)
- 2 Samuel 11:2-17, 26-27; 12:1-7: David and Nathan—Challenging Abuses of Power (Changing Stories)
- Jeremiah 22:13-17: Jeremiah and Jehoiakim—To Know God Is to Do Justice (Changing Priorities)
- Daniel 3:1-18: Furnaces and Faith—"But If Not . . ." (Unchanging Allegiance)
- Matthew 25:31-46: Jesus' Vision—A Task for the Nations (Changing the Answer)
- Luke 1:46-55: Mary's Song—Whom Do We Hear? (Changing Perspectives)
- Luke 4:16-30: Jesus at Nazareth—Good News to the Poor (Changing Structures)
- Luke 9:28-43: Transfiguration—Ecstasy and Epilepsy (Changing Location)
- Luke 10:25-37: Jesus' Story—From Head Trips to Foot Trips (Changing the Question)
- Luke 24:13-35: Emmaus . . . and Back Again—A New Way of Knowing (Changing Stories)

After each group has taken one of the passages above and discussed it, the larger group will come together to discuss the connection between these passages and our understanding of Christian stewardship. Consider how stewardship of our personal and collective resources shapes our relationships with one another as Christians.

Then ask participants the following questions:

- How is stewardship of our money a spiritual discipline?
- How might we preach and teach stewardship effectively in a congregation?
- Which scriptures focus on stewardship?
- What is the goal of stewardship in the Bible?

Further Biblical Exploration. Invite the class to form two groups. Ask one group to read Deuteronomy 10:17-18 and the other group to read Amos 8:4-8. Invite each group to consider the passage in light of the Economic Community section in the *Social Principles*. How might this section change the way we understand the church's ministry and mission?

Read the "Covenant Prayer in the Wesleyan Tradition" together:

I am no longer my own, but thine.
Put me to what thou wilt, rank me with whom thou wilt.
Put me to doing, put me to suffering.
Let me be employed by thee or laid aside for thee,
exalted for thee or brought low by thee.
Let me be full, let me be empty.
Let me have all things, let me have nothing.
I freely and heartily yield all things
to thy pleasure and disposal.
And now, O glorious and blessed God,
Father, Son, and Holy Spirit,
thou art mine, and I am thine. So be it.
And the covenant which I have made on earth,
let it be ratified in heaven. Amen.[5]

Session Review and Assignments (5 Minutes). Ask for volunteers to lead the closing worship for the next session. Tell participants to read the section on the Political Community in the *Social Principles* booklet.

Closing Prayer (5 Minutes)

"A Worker's Prayer"

My Lord, Jesus Christ
I offer You, this day,
all my work, my hopes and struggles,
my joys and sorrows.
Grant me, and all my fellow workers,
the grace to think like You,
to work with You,
and to live in You.
Help me to love You with all my heart,
and to serve You with all my strength.
Lord, Jesus Christ, Carpenter of Nazareth,
You were a worker as I am.
Give me, and all workers, the privilege
to work as You did,
so that everything we do
will be to the greater glory of God,
and the benefit of our fellow men.
May Your kingdom come into our offices,
our factories and shops,
into our homes and into our streets.
Give us this day a living wage,
so that we may be able to keep Your law.
May we earn it without envy or injustice.
To us who labor and are heavily burdened,
send speedily the refreshment of Your love.
May we never sin against You.

Show us Your way to work,
and when our work here is done,
may we, with all our fellow workers,
rest in peace.
Amen.[6]

God of justice, manifest in a carpenter's son
We pray for all who labor and toil
And for those charged with protecting the conditions of their work.
Grant to these stewards of economic justice
An abiding and untiring commitment to the rights of workers
And to the protection of international labor standards throughout the world.

—Anonymous worker's prayer[7]

Part One: The Political Community

Learning Goals

- To understand more about the church's position on politics
- To develop thoughts on what the scriptures say about the world community and political community
- To discern if one feels called to be an advocate for the most vulnerable in our society and in our world
- To see that God's world is a complex place
- To realize the need for the gospel in our changing world

Preparation

You will need a glass of water, a bowl of sand, and a chalkboard or flip chart. Write the following passages of scripture on index cards, one passage per card: Luke 4:16-19; Luke 23:20-25; Luke 23:32-34; John 8:1-11; Acts 21:30-36. Review the "Politics—A Dirty Word" and "Concentric Circles" exercises ahead of time.

Session Plan

Opening Worship (10 Minutes). Introduce the "Prayer of John Chrysostom" (*UMH*, no. 412) by describing how it offers a beautiful pattern for prayer. Invite the group to pray it aloud. Ask for prayer concerns from the class and continue in prayer. You may also read aloud 1 Peter 2:1-5. Then read or sing the words of "Dear Lord, Lead Me Day by Day" (*UMH*, no. 411).

Review (5 Minutes). Ask participants if they have questions from the previous session.

Explore the Political Principles (10 Minutes). The instructor may offer all or some of these observations, realizing that time is limited and everything might not be touched upon. The leader should of course take special care in dealing with issues most relevant to the group's needs and contexts.

- **Violence repels us, but violence also attracts us.** Violence alarms us, but violence also entertains us. Violence destroys us, but violence also protects us. Is violence inevitable? Why do people use violence?

- **Violence is employed to make others serve our own self-interests.** Slavery may be the most obvious example of this, and for many people slavery has yet to be abolished. In Jesus' day, and in the early church, slavery was legal. For Christians, however, slavery was considered immoral and antithetical to the abundant life demonstrated in the example of Jesus. We do not have to institutionalize slavery to produce the kind of relationship where one person, or a group of people, is thought to exist only to serve the needs and self-interests of another person or group. What alternative vision of interdependence do the Social Principles offer?

- **Violence is used to make others resemble us.** We use violence to make others conform to our own beliefs and behaviors. Social and economic systems commit acts of violence against entire cultures. What alternative vision to this kind of violence do the Social Principles offer?

- **Violence is used to steal from others.** We are caught in global economic relation-ships that violate many to the benefit of a few. Wars are fought over diamonds, water, land, and oil. What alternative vision of stewardship of God's creation do the Social Principles offer?

- **Violence is used to punish offenders.** When people are given the choice of what to do with those who are accused of crime, their first reaction is usually that they should be punished. What alternative vision of justice do the Social Principles offer?

- **Violence is used to protect us.** This is the issue that those who think violence is inevitable use as their proof. Whatever a person or a community may or may not do in a particular context, the use of violence is self-defeating in the long term. (See the publication by the Council of Bishops, *In Search of Security.*) What alternative vision of personal and communal security do the Social Principles offer?

Invite the class to form five groups. Assign each group one of the sections from the Social Principles listed below (¶164). Ask the groups to read and then discuss the sections they have been assigned.

Group 1 — (¶164.A) Basic Freedoms and Human Rights; (¶164.B) Political Responsibility
Group 2 — (¶164.C) Church and State Relations; (¶164.D) Freedom of Information
Group 3 — (¶164.E) Education; (¶164.F) Civil Obedience and Civil Disobedience
Group 4 — (¶164.G) The Death Penalty; (¶164.H) Criminal and Restorative Justice
Group 5 — (¶164.I) Military Service

Invite each group to paraphrase the sections they were assigned and discuss the subjects' relevance within their congregations.

Have each group report its discussion to the class. Explain that this section of the Social Principles deals directly with pursuing responsible political life. Invite the group to identify the principle in today's session that would be the most difficult to implement in today's society.

Exploring Justice from a Biblical Point of View (10 Minutes). Move into small groups to read these biblical passages: Amos 5:11-12 and 5:21-24; Luke 4:16-19; 23:20-25; and 23:32-34; John 8:1-11; Acts 21:30-36.

After participants summarize the readings, ask the class the following questions:

- Why does God hate Israel's religious feasts, offerings, and music?
- Does this righteous anger surprise us? Why or why not?
- What does God say is more important than these ritual ceremonies?
- What would the world be like if justice flowed as Amos describes?

Exploring Justice through Sand and Water (5 Minutes). Bruce Feiler wrote a best-selling book titled *Walking the Bible: A Journey by Land through the Five Books of Moses.*[8] In the book, Feiler describes his travels to the places named in the Bible and discusses water and its importance in the Middle East.

Pass a bowl of sand around the group, and ask participants to let the sand flow through their fingers and notice how it feels. Invite the class to imagine living in a desert area and walking in dry sand every day without water nearby.

Once everyone has completed the activity, pass a glass of water around the group. Instruct participants to dip a finger into the water, name something they do with water, and then pass it to the next person. Ask participants to avoid repeating a use named by another person.

Discuss the biblical significance of water. For example, water is an important part of life for desert-dwelling people. It is important for us too, but we often take it for granted. Most of us can get water whenever we want by turning on a faucet or from a water fountain. Water is vital for life and an economic and political commodity.

Invite a volunteer to read Amos 5:21-24 aloud. Ask the class to respond to the phrase "let justice roll on like a river, righteousness like a never-failing stream" (NIV) and what that phrase means to them. How might water flow in a desert?

After discussion, you might say: "God wants justice to be as important to people as water, and God wants justice to be as strong as the rains that flood Israel in the winter. Do you think that today in our community and society we worry about justice as much as God does and as much as God wants us to?"

Retributive and Restorative Justice (10 Minutes). Introduce these concepts with the following statement: "Our current criminal justice system in the United States is primarily retributive. If someone commits a crime, he or she is incarcerated. We cast him or her from society. We ignore his or her humanity, often letting them be defined by one act." Continue by saying, "Another type of justice, *restorative*, involves forgiveness and repentance. Its purpose is to heal the people affected by crime—both victim and offender. The term *restorative* comes from the word *restore*. Restorative justice restores the peace and wholeness of a community after a crime has been committed. America's prison system does use certain principles of restorative justice, namely by helping some persons who have been convicted of crimes reenter society through education and rehabilitation."

Write the scripture passages below on index cards, one per card. Invite participants to gather in small groups and identify which type of criminal justice—retributive or restorative—is present in the text:

- Luke 23:32-34 (Both retributive—Jesus' execution; and restorative—Jesus' statement, "Father, forgive them; for they do not know what they are doing." Whichever way the class prefers to look at it will work, but point out how there are examples of both present in the text. The cross is both a means of torture and a sign of God's overcoming violence and using it as a way to bring salvation to a fallen humanity.)

- Luke 4:16-19 (Restorative: Jesus calls for prisoners to be freed and the oppressed to be released.)
- Luke 23:20-25 (Retributive: The crowd shouts for Jesus' crucifixion, and Pilate gives in.)
- John 8:1-11 (Restorative: Jesus doesn't condemn the woman for committing adultery, but instead forgives her.)
- Acts 21:30-36 (Retributive: Paul is beaten and arrested for spreading the gospel.)

After this exercise, ask participants:

- Is the notion of justice in the Bible consistent throughout all of scripture?
- Does the idea of justice exemplified by Jesus and the early Christians differ from that of most people in the world today?
- What are some examples in today's world that are against the kind of justice Jesus calls for?

Conclude this section by saying to the class, "When Jesus was alive, he was very different from the mainstream society. He thought society needed to be turned around. He spoke about God's vision of shalom (peace with justice). As Christians, how important is it to speak out against wrong? If we don't, who will?"

Exercise: Politics—A Dirty Word? (10 Minutes). Some Christians believe that faith and politics do not go together. If this is the case, we may need to redefine both *politics* and *faith*.

This exercise is a way for participants to examine what the Bible teaches about their beliefs on particular social issues. It is most helpful when it follows a discussion of faith and political beliefs.

For example, you might ask participants the following questions:

- What do you think of when you hear the term *politics* or *political*? What does the dictionary say about the origin of these terms?
- Jesus spoke of the Holy Spirit as an "advocate" or a "spirit of truth" that God was sending to humanity. What does it mean to you to be an advocate?
- How is an advocate different from a lobbyist?

- Are the political beliefs of most Christians you know essentially the same as the beliefs of the rest of the community (or state or nation) or radically different? Why do you think this is the case?
- What do you think Jesus would say about the current political discourse in your community, town, state, or the country as a whole?
- What do you think Jesus would say about what is represented as "Christian" political belief?

It is important to show how the logic for the Social Principles is shaped by biblical teaching. Understanding that the Social Principles are rooted in scripture may ease the tension that can result from disagreement over social policies as they are determined by any state.

It may be helpful to illustrate this exercise with the following example, adapted from Eric Sapp and Mara Vanderslice's article, "Policy Maker's Guide to Poverty, Social Justice, and the Prophetic Voice in the Bible."[9]

Read Isaiah 58:2-7 to the class, or invite a volunteer to do so. Ask the class what they think this passage of scripture means. Why is God displeased? Where does this passage fit within the six categories into which the Social Principles are divided (Natural World, Nurturing Community, Social Community, Economic Community, Political Community, and World Community)?

Once participants have contributed to the general discussion around the meaning of these scriptures for them, they may begin to feel more comfortable with small-group work. Due to time constraints, it is helpful for participants to form five small groups that correspond to the five community sections of the *Social Principles* booklet. Participants will then be able to concentrate on one area of social policy as dictated by the leader or group consensus.

Invite participants to form five groups. Ask each group to write a statement about the position taken by The United Methodist Church on one of the topics listed below. Ask participants to support their positions with scripture passages from the Bible.

Group 1 — (¶164) Functions of Government; Elections; Capital Punishment; Slavery

Group 2 — (¶164) Citizen Participation; Separation of Church and State; Ethical Influence of the Church

Group 3 — (¶164) Public Schools; Prayer in Schools; Civil Disobedience/Obedience; Restorative Justice versus Retributive Justice

Group 4 — (¶164) War; Enforced Military Service (the Draft); Conscientious Objectors; Military Service

Group 5 — (¶165) United Nations; Use of National Power; Technology

Discuss the following question: Can the church be political without being partisan? Invite participants to move beyond yes or no responses to offer reasons as to whether the church can witness politically without being partisan.

Break (5 Minutes). Allow a short break to shift gears and prepare to dig more deeply into the content.

Part Two: The World Community

Spiritual Disciplines (20 Minutes). Read and discuss the first paragraph of ¶165 in the *Social Principles* booklet. Invite the group to discuss examples of the complexity of life today. Ask the group to consider how the Social Principles seek to address the complex issues with which we are faced today.

Select two volunteers to read Acts 17:26 and 1 Peter 2:9 aloud. Ask how these two scripture passages connect with concepts expressed in the *Social Principles* concerning the world community. Ask the class the following question: What examples can you give in which international cooperation by governments or by nongovernmental groups has made a definite advance in improving the world community?

Invite the class to form five groups. Invite each group to read one of the following paragraphs from the *Social Principles of The United Methodist Church*:

Group 1 — (¶165) First paragraph (introduction)
Group 2 — (¶165.A) Nations and Cultures
Group 3 — (¶165.B) National Power and Responsibility
Group 4 — (¶165.C) War and Peace
Group 5 — (¶165.D) Justice and Law

Invite each group to ask questions and identify their thoughts, feelings, and reactions to the paragraphs they have just read. Participants may choose to draw or write a response in their journals.

Ask each group to report on their conversations by identifying the paragraph they were assigned and any insights they gleaned.

Explain to the class that in the year 303 CE, the emperor Diocletian forbade any member of the Roman army to be a Christian. By the year 416 CE, no one could be a member of the

Roman army unless he was a Christian. After Constantine legalized Christianity in 313 CE, exceptional conviction was required to be a Christian and not support the military.

This called forth a new development, namely, the doctrine of the invisibility of the church. After Constantine, people assumed as a fact that God was governing history through the emperor and his military. Jumping forward to 1757, Wesley denounced war as evil. In 1781, Charles Wesley parodied war in hymns. In 1928 the Methodist Church declared the following:

> We would utterly repudiate our professed faith in our Lord Jesus Christ the Prince of Peace if we held that war is inevitable. Disputes among nations like disputes between individuals may be settled by judicial processes. We believe therefore that war should be made a public crime under the law of nations.[10]

Exercise: Concentric Circles (25 Minutes). This exercise in communication begins with the belief that individuals have a deep desire to speak from their own experiences and to be heard without judgment or condemnation. Persons become fully engaged in community when they are asked to voice their positions, interests, values, perceptions, and needs. In the process, persons are affirmed and feel appreciated.

In this exercise, participants are asked to disclose their experiences, biases, beliefs, and uncertainties. The questions asked in this exercise are intentionally open-ended; there are no right or wrong answers.

This exercise should be a time for sharing new insights in a safe environment. Some participants may shift their perspectives and affirm experiences quite different from those they once held. The Concentric Circles exercise may increase a participant's ability to actively listen for common threads of action, and to speak with conviction and without fear.

Establish ground rules before beginning the exercise to increase a sense of respect, tolerance, and safety among participants. One ground rule is to show respect for everyone at all times during and after the exercise.

Set up the exercise:

1. Invite the class to stand as they are able and form a circle. Ask participants to count off in twos. Invite the "twos" to take a step to the center of the circle and join hands. Invite the "ones" to remain in place and join hands. Ask the inner circle to turn and face the outer. Ask the circles

to shake hands and introduce themselves. An even number of participants is required for this exercise to work best. If there is an odd number of participants, ask that people work in threes.

2. Those in the inner circle will be the first to speak. Ask participants to speak without editing their responses. Ask them to use "I" statements and to speak based on their own experiences, perspectives, beliefs, values, feelings, and thoughts. Ask those who listen to do so with their ears, not with their mouths.

3. After one minute, each pair should switch roles. Those who listened will now answer the same question, and those who spoke will now listen. At the end of each two-minute conversation, ask those in the outer circle to move to the right and meet a new partner from the inner circle.

Once the class understands the exercise, the leader should read a statement from the Concentric Circles exercise aloud as found in the *Social Principles* booklet. Allow approximately two minutes for each pair to respond to the statement. Then invite the outer circle to move to the right and read another statement from this section. Continue through the list of statements.

At the end of this exercise, take time to process feelings and thoughts by asking the following questions:

- How did it feel to speak without interruption?
- What was it like to listen without interrupting or responding?
- Which statements challenged you?
- Which statements seemed easy to discuss? Why?
- Was anyone surprised by an answer they gave or by an answer they heard?
- What was the point of this exercise?

An alternative exercise is to look at the Millennium Development Goals (MDGs), which are benchmarks the community of nations has agreed to try to achieve by 2015. The MDGs flesh out many of the statements found in the World Community section of the *Social Principles*. Consider each of the MDGs individually or as a whole.

1. **Eradicate extreme poverty and hunger.** The number of underweight children in the world declined from 31 percent to 26 percent between 1990 and 2008 in rural areas and the developing world. More children are breast-feeding around the world, leading to reduced child mortality.

2. **Achieve universal primary education.** Primary school is attended by 84 percent of the world's children, but 100 million remain out of school. The largest gaps in education based on gender are in sub-Saharan Africa, South Asia, Latin America, and the Caribbean.

3. **Promote gender equality and empower women.** "About two thirds of countries and territories reached gender parity in primary education by the target year of 2005. But in many countries—especially in sub-Saharan Africa and South Asia—girls are still at a disadvantage."

4. **Reduce child mortality.** Between 1990 and 2008, infant mortality fell by 28 percent. But the disparity in child survival rates remains high in sub-Saharan Africa, and many of these deaths could be prevented, just as the deaths of 2.5 million children have already been prevented due to immunizations.

5. **Improve maternal health.** For every woman who dies during childbirth in sub-Saharan Africa, approximately twenty women suffer from injury, infection, disease, or disability as a result of complications of pregnancy and childbirth.

6. **Combat HIV/AIDS, malaria, and other diseases.** An estimated 33.4 million people worldwide live with AIDS. Of this number, 2.1 million are children under the age of fifteen.

7. **Ensure environmental sustainability.** Clean drinking water is reaching more people than ever and sanitation facilities have improved; however, 884 million people still lack clean drinking water.

8. **Develop a global partnership for development.** "Official development assistance stood at $126 billion in 2012. A total of 83 percent of least developed country exports enter developed countries duty-free. Trade of developing countries and transition economies outpaced the world average. . . . In the developing world, 31 percent of the population use the Internet, compared with 77 percent of the developed world."[11]

How do the Millennium Development Goals and the World Community section of the Social Principles align with the gospel of Jesus Christ?

Session Review and Assignments (5 Minutes). Ask participants to read "Our First Social Creed of the Methodist Church" and the biblical foundations sections in the *Social Principles* in preparation for the next session. Request volunteers to lead the opening worship for the next session.

Closing Prayer (5 Minutes). Invite a volunteer to close with prayer. Before the closing prayer, invite the group to offer petitions related to the topics discussed in this session.

Session Five

Part One: Our First Social Creed

Learning Goals

- To understand our Social Creed
- To understand from where our church has come and how it has been shaped by the Social Creed
- To understand how the Bible informs the Social Creed and the Social Principles
- To suggest resources for further study and reflection
- To better understand what can be done to promote the Social Principles in the church

Preparation

Write both the original and the current Social Creeds on sheets of newsprint. Display the newsprint so that it is visible to everyone in the class. Bring to the session pictures of social and political issues addressed in one or both of the creeds. Review the 1908 Social Creed found in the introduction to the Social Principles section.

Session Plan

Opening Worship (10 Minutes). Ask for prayer concerns from the class. Pray for the concerns offered; then join together in praying "For Direction" (*UMH*, no. 705). Join in praise by reading aloud Psalm 37:1-11 (*UMH*, no. 772). Read Isaiah 41:10-13 aloud, and speak about the importance of the phrase "Do not fear" in this passage.

Ask participants the following questions:

- Does an image or a picture come to you after hearing this passage?
- How might this passage help you deal with a particular issue in your life or community?
- What does this passage call you to do, to be, or to change?

Review (5 Minutes). Ask participants if they have questions from the previous session.

Spiritual Practice (25 Minutes). Read the current Social Creed (1972), followed by the 1908 Social Creed. Compare the language in the two creeds. Invite participants to think about what was happening in 1908 that was similar to our time as well as what was different. Discuss what has changed in our culture and what remains the same. (Expect a lively conversation!)

Explain the following:

> A young Irish girl named Maureen began work at age 14 in a woolen mill in Lawrence, Massachusetts. Starting at six o'clock every morning she swept and cleaned the mill floor. Maureen was paid $3.50 for this (a fifty-six-hour week), ten cents of which went for drinking water from a polluted canal. While working, she saw many older workers seriously injured by the dangerous mill machinery because they were forced to work so fast. Maureen and her family had left Ireland to escape famine, and they all lived in one room in a boarding house. Each day lunch and supper consisted of black bread, molasses, and beans. On Sunday hopefully there was a piece of meat.[12]

Our Social Creed originated more than one hundred years ago to express outrage over the numerous factories, mines, mills, tenements, and company towns whose workers and residents, like Maureen, paid the human cost of rapid industrialization and growing prosperity of the United States.

Workers were caught in the machinery of early industrialization and ground down by fourteen-hour shifts and seven-day workweeks. Families were torn apart by absent or exhausted parents. Those disabled were summarily dismissed. Retired workers were left without pensions. Children worked when they should have been at school or at play. At the same time, the owners of industry generated enormous wealth.

The Social Gospel movement, evangelical at its heart and inspired by Jesus' preaching of the kingdom of God, was acutely aware of the brutalities of new working conditions, the social tensions of millions of European immigrants moving to the United States, and the loss of communal values in fast-growing cities. The Social Gospel movement advocated for a more responsible democracy; for a day of Sabbath, a living wage, an end to sweatshop labor, and recognition of human rights across class divides. This movement took seriously the effects not only of personal sin but also of social sin. The ethicist Reinhold Niebuhr, who was affected by the Social Gospel movement, put it well: "Man's capacity for justice makes democracy possible; but man's inclination to injustice makes democracy necessary."[13]

Inspired by the recent organization in England of the Wesleyan Methodist Union and the community-organizing efforts of Methodist suffragettes Jane Addams and Mary McDowell, five Methodist Episcopal clergy formed the Methodist Federation for Social Service: New York Conference evangelist Frank Mason North, who authored the Methodist hymn "Where Cross the Crowded Ways of Life"; Ohio Wesleyan University president Herbert Welch; publishing house editor Elbert Robb Zaring; and Cleveland pastor Worth Tippy and Chicago pastor Harry F. Ward, both of whom had conducted many untimely funerals for packinghouse workers killed in factory accidents.

Deuteronomy 30:14 says, "The word is very near to you; it is in your mouth and in your heart for you to observe." Social witness statements have been a prominent part of our faith heritage.

The 1908 Social Creed states, "The Methodist Episcopal Church stands for . . . the mind of Christ as the supreme law of society and the sure remedy for all social ills." First drafted on a Western Union notepad, its eleven-point platform was adopted without dissent on May 30, 1908, by the General Conference meeting in Baltimore. One-fourth of the episcopal address was devoted to social issues, especially those involving child labor and the union movement.

Subsequently, the Social Creed was presented at the White House to President Theodore Roosevelt. Thoroughly Wesleyan and ecumenical, within two years the Federal Council of Churches—now the National Council of Churches of Christ in the USA—would adopt the Social Creed as its own.

The new Social Creed quickly became a public rallying point for our church and was memorized by a generation of new converts to Methodism. More than one hundred years later it is still part of our Methodist DNA. It symbolizes the intent of The United Methodist Church to proclaim the urgency of the gospel and to hold persons and institutions accountable for change.

The 1908 Social Creed attempted to "threaten the world with resurrection." Bishop Sharon Brown Christopher charged the church to do that at the 2008 General Conference.

The 1908 Social Creed expressed deep and powerful distress over the plight of the working poor and the rights of laborers, the need for improved working conditions, and a call for the abolition of child labor. The Social Creed was a public pledge to work together for a fairer and more faithful church and society.

Language is important. There are two small words in English worth noting—*to* and *for*. Doing something *to* someone is generally understood as having power over him. Standing *for* something or someone suggests a deeper level of solidarity. The 1908 Social Creed avoided the paternalistic "to" language and favored standing "for" and with people.

The 1908 Social Creed signaled to the political powers and principalities of the day that in a highly individualistic culture, Christian faithfulness must be social as well as personal. It moved the church beyond a preoccupation solely with ministries of mercy, which cause us to empathize with the poor and marginalized, to an organized engagement with justice, which requires us to be advocates on their behalf.

But the 1908 Social Creed was not perfect and omitted several key movements of the day. We need to remember that racial justice was an issue largely ignored in status quo national-level politics, although a number of Protestant leaders were deeply involved with desegregation efforts in the schools and colleges that their home mission boards supported in the South. The global South and Europe were absent from the drafting of the document.

The 1908 Social Creed foreshadowed the church's ongoing critique of abuse of privileges. It held firm to the belief that dignity is God's gift to humanity and our obligation to one another is justice: forming decisions to do what is right before God and neighbor by meeting human needs and pursuing structural justice.

Addictions to alcohol and gambling were not mentioned. Gender equity was also absent. Recognition and affirmation of our sacred worth and sexual identity, threats to ecological sustainability, responsible corporate investment, and life in an age of mass communication, to name a few issues, were all still on the horizon.

Examine the 1908 Social Creed:

1. Review each of the six individual items.
2. Define the major focus for all six items.

3. Ask about the social conditions in 1908 that may have shaped these. Statistical information is provided below.

4. Conclude by asking the following questions:

- What do you think is the major focus of all the items in the 1908 Social Creed?
- How would this older creed apply or not apply to today's world?

Consider the context in which the 1908 Social Creed was written. Share these statistics for 1904:

- The average life expectancy in the United States was forty-seven years.
- Only 14 percent of homes in the United States had a bathtub.
- Only 8 percent of the homes had a telephone.
- A three-minute call from Denver to New York City cost $11.
- There were only eight thousand cars in the United States, and only 144 miles of paved roads.
- The speed limit in most cities was 10 mph.
- Alabama, Mississippi, Iowa, and Tennessee were each more heavily populated than California, the twenty-first most populous state.
- The tallest structure in the world was the Eiffel Tower.
- The average wage in the United States was twenty-two cents an hour.
- The average US worker made between $200 and $400 per year.
- A competent accountant could expect to earn $2,000 per year; a dentist $2,500 per year; a veterinarian between $1,500 and $4,000 per year; and a mechanical engineer about $5,000 per year.
- More than 95 percent of all births in the United States took place at home.
- Ninety percent of physicians in the United States had no college education. Instead, they attended medical schools, many of which were condemned in the press and by the government as "substandard."
- Sugar cost four cents a pound, eggs were fourteen cents a dozen, and coffee was fifteen cents a pound.
- Most women washed their hair only once a month and used borax or egg yolk as shampoo.
- Canada passed a law prohibiting "poor people" from entering the country for any reason.

- The six leading causes of death in the United States were pneumonia and influenza, tuberculosis, diarrhea, heart disease, and stroke.
- The American flag had forty-five stars. Arizona, New Mexico, Hawaii, and Alaska had not been admitted to the Union yet.
- The population of Las Vegas, Nevada, was thirty people.
- Crossword puzzles, canned beer, and iced tea had not been invented.
- There was no Mother's Day or Father's Day.
- Two out of every ten adults in the United States could not read or write.
- Only 6 percent of all Americans had graduated high school.
- Marijuana, heroin, and morphine were available over the counter at corner drugstores.
- Eighteen percent of US households had at least one full-time servant or domestic.
- There were approximately 230 reported murders in the entire United States.

Read our current Social Creed in the *Social Principles* booklet aloud to the class, and then ask the questions below:

1. Does our current creed cover all of the Social Principles? Is anything missing? Does it contain too much?
2. What suggestions do you have for improvements?
3. How does the current creed compare to the Apostles' Creed and the Nicene Creed?
4. How can we make the Social Creed more well-known and used in the church?
5. What do you think about the recommendation that it be frequently used in Sunday worship? How would your congregation respond if the Social Creed were used monthly or quarterly in your church?
6. How do you think the global church outside the United States would resonate with the issues named in the 1908 Social Creed and the current Social Creed?

Then and Now: Compare the Two Creeds (20 Minutes). Invite participants to read both creeds aloud. Ask them to identify particular concerns or affirmations in each creed. Ask the class to gather in pairs and to note and discuss the historical issues that challenged the church and society during both periods. What groups of people are named? What groups are absent? What social, economic, political, and cultural issues are named? What issues are absent? How would you account for the issues that are absent?

Discuss whether the concerns of the 1908 Social Creed are still valid today. What shape do they take in the twenty-first century? Which concerns call for acts of mercy and which call for acts of justice?

Invite participants to tape images or pictures that illustrate the concerns next to the section each creed addresses. Invite participants to describe why they chose these images and their own connections to the concerns.

Ask participants to read the current Social Creed quietly and prayerfully, and then reflect and journal on their own lives in the Creed by answering the following questions:

- Where do they see themselves in the Social Creed?
- Where do they see their congregations, communities, nations, and world in the Social Creed?
- What words of concern or affirmation are missing for them in the Social Creed?

Ask participants to imagine themselves two hundred years into the future and answer the following questions:

- What language would they incorporate into a global United Methodist Social Creed for the twenty-third century?
- What would this Social Creed have in common with the 1908 Social Creed?
- How would it be distinctive?
- What would it have in common with ecumenical confessions of faith around issues of justice?

Finally, compare the 1908 Social Creed and the current Social Creed with the Apostles' Creed, the Nicene Creed, and the 2008 Companion Litany to the Social Creed. Ask participants the following questions:

- What images are similar and dissimilar in each?
- What role did each play for the church in its day?
- What distinctive voice of faith does the United Methodist Social Creed contribute to our ethical and theological development?
- What images of creation and grace, sin and salvation, slavery and deliverance, and the unity of the Trinity and the unity of humanity do the creeds reflect?
- How does this influence our ethical actions in and for the world?

Challenge participants to think of ways to use the creed in worship other than recitation. For example, could portions of the Social Creed be used as calls to worship? Prayers of confession? Invitations to discipleship?

Break (5 Minutes). Allow a short break to shift gears and prepare to dig more deeply into the content.

Part Two: Biblical Foundations for the Social Principles

A Brief Review and a Look Ahead (5 Minutes). Ask participants to name ways the Social Creed might be used in their congregations.

Reflection (10 Minutes). Remind participants that as lay servants they can interact with the Social Creed, the Social Principles, and the 2008 Companion Litany to the Social Creed as living embodiments of the church of Jesus Christ and the people called United Methodist.

What do we mean by reflection? Dr. Fred Smith, a professor at Wesley Theological Seminary in Washington, D.C., reminds us that the word *reflection* is based on two words: *re* and *flex*—"to bend again."

Ask the class if anyone has ever visited a house of mirrors in an amusement park. When you look at yourself in a house of mirrors, you may appear thin, fat, tall, or skinny. You are the same person, but you see yourself differently. The bending light waves and different shapes of mirrors determine what you do and do not see.

Similarly, our vision as United Methodists is shaped by several mirrors: biblical heritage, culture, local church, vocation or profession, economic status, and gender.

When we look at an event in society, it is as if we are looking at a mirror in a house of mirrors. We not only look at the event; we also look at ourselves. How shall we respond to the event? Our actions will be determined by whom we see reflected in the mirror. Our response to an event, a crisis, or an opportunity depends on who we see ourselves to be. We will interpret an event differently based on how we see that event reflected back on ourselves.

Often it is hard to tell which image is the accurate one. Reflection is a theological art. The Social Principles give us permission to look at the same set of problems from different perspectives.

Explore Biblical Foundations of the Social Principles (20 Minutes). Invite the class to form six groups. Ask each group to respond to the topics and corresponding questions below:

- **Group 1 — ¶160. The Natural World:** Name the six general groups of Social Principles. What beliefs do you hold about God that would help you engage in social witness? What two beliefs can be found in the first paragraph? Read Genesis 1:26-30. What responsibilities do we have toward creation? List ways in which the Social Principles support the natural world.

- **Group 2 — ¶161. The Nurturing Community:** Review the general topics. Read Acts 2:43-47 and 11:1-18. How do these scripture passages relate to the nurturing community? How do they speak to the church today? Imagine that you live in a community and culture different from your own. Name that place and think about how you might live as a Christian there.

- **Group 3 — ¶162. The Social Community:** Read Matthew 11:2-6 aloud. Journal about your reflections on this passage in the context of the Social Principles. How does this passage relate to the ministry of your church? Over past decades, General Conference has added new sections to the Social Community paragraph. Do you have any suggestions for this section?

- **Group 4 — ¶163. The Economic Community:** Read Deuteronomy 10:17-18 and Amos 8:4-8. How do these connect with the Social Principles concerning the economic community? If you took the Social Principles on this topic seriously, what economic changes would you make?

- **Group 5 — ¶164. The Political Community:** Read 1 Peter 2:17. Discuss the meaning of "political responsibility" and what it would look like in practice. Give examples that illustrate appropriate civil disobedience. Discuss your understanding of the separation of church and state.

- **Group 6 — ¶165. The World Community:** Read Acts 17:26 and 1 Peter 2:9. How do these scripture passages connect with our understanding of the world community? Name examples in which governments or other groups have improved the world community. As globalization increasingly becomes a reality, and The United Methodist Church expands across the globe, are there other issues you think our church may want to address in this section?

Reconvene the class and have each group speak on its discussion and findings.

Resources (5 Minutes). Tell participants about the following resources. You may also direct them to the "Resources" section in the *Social Principles* booklet. If possible, have an example of each to show the class:

- *Social Principles* in Spanish and Korean
- *Social Principles* bulletin inserts
- *Living Our Principles*—a six-part film series on the Social Principles produced by the General Board of Church and Society
- Information about the United Methodist Seminar Program on National and International Affairs is also available from the General Board of Church and Society, 100 Maryland Ave. NE, Washington, DC 20002. www.umc-gbcs.org.

Session Review/Evaluation (5 Minutes). Ask participants to complete course evaluations before they leave. The instructor might ask:

- What went well for you in the course?
- What would you change in the course?
- What difference will this course make in your life and in the life of your congregation?

Closing Worship (10 Minutes). Invite those who volunteered to lead the opening worship to begin this time together. After closing worship, consider distributing certificates to those who have completed the course. Include words of appreciation for their participation in the course. You may convene all classes for worship or for the presentation of certificates or for any other closing that your district committee has established. Your district or conference lay servant committee may want to recognize non–lay servants who completed this course with a special recognition program.

APPENDIX
ADDITIONAL INFORMATION
FOR THE LEADER

Practice healthy dialogue. *Dialogue* is often confused with *argument*. We generally think of argument as having winners and losers, and points are made for the sake of winning. In dialogue, we seek new solutions that may use the best of both positions to articulate a creative alternative. Here are some practices for healthy dialogue: Increase your own intellectual, spiritual, and emotional curiosity. Ask open-ended questions that begin with words like *why, how, who,* and *when.* Listen to understand and speak to be understood. Listen with your heart, head, and spirit. Know where you stand and take a risk to explain your position.

Respect different perceptions and opinions. Check to make sure that what you hear is accurate. Sometimes you may need to respond to another person by saying, "If I hear you correctly, then you are saying . . . ," and restate the other person's ideas.

Practice objectivity. Suspend judgments and use language that explains and describes your own experience. Ask for clarity when needed. Avoid pretending to know what you do not know.

Amnesty. Practice forgiveness and understand that perceptions change based on new experiences and insights.

Relocate. Try to see the world through the eyes of a person whose social status or access to privilege in society is different from your own.

Use value, feeling, and needs language. Look and listen for common and different values, feelings, and needs when you find yourself in disagreement.

Build alliances. Confront attitudes and behaviors that perpetuate division based on race, gender, or economics. Validate attitudes and behaviors that demonstrate respect and tolerance for all people.

Let go of the need for specific outcomes. Allow for some level of confusion and ambiguity. Look for and brainstorm common ground and common actions in the midst of disagreements. Explain and explore consequences.

Remember what John Wesley said on having a catholic spirit. John Wesley preached often and wrote extensively. He stood for Christian practice, and he expected to see warm hearts in action. What follows is from a pamphlet Wesley wrote concerning the "catholic [or universal] spirit":

> It is certain, so long as we know but *in part,* that all men will not see all things alike. It is an unavoidable consequence of the present weakness and shortness of human understanding, that several men will be of several minds in religion as well as in common life. So it has been from the beginning of the world, and so it will be "till the restitution of all things." . . . Every wise man, therefore, will allow others the same liberty of thinking which he desires they should allow him; and will no more insist on their embracing his opinions, than he would have them to insist on his embracing theirs. He bears with those who differ from him, and only asks him with whom he desires to unite in love that single question, "Is thy heart right, as my heart is with thy heart?"[14]

For Wesley, rightness of heart was far more important than rightness of doctrinal subtleties.

Use the Circle Process and respectful dialogue. To understand the Social Principles, we must think theologically. Go ahead; be challenged; be comforted; be uplifted; be moved by the Holy Spirit; get closer to God; be closer to Jesus Christ and closer to his body.

In discussions on contemporary topics, we may find ourselves on either side of any given issue. In such cases, we need to practice respectful dialogue through a healthful method known as the "Circle Process." (The Concentric Circle exercise used in this course is a step toward this process.) Begin with enough chairs in a circle for all participants. There should be no extra chairs in the circle. Hold up a Bible or a feather, a stick, or any small physical object that can be held by each person. Explain that this object is the talking piece that will be passed around the circle. The person who receives the talking piece is the only one who should talk. Others should listen until the talking piece is passed to them.

Follow these guidelines for using the Circle Process. Personal information shared in the circle is kept confidential, and nothing will be shared outside of the classroom unless the leader feels it is necessary to do so (for example, if safety might be compromised). The goal is to allow space for all participants in the circle to speak honestly and without fear of judgment, and to practice the art of listening to understand another person's perspective as that person presents it.

- Speak with respect.
- Use statements that begin with "I" ("I think," "I feel," "I believe," and so on) rather than statements that begin with "You."
- Be specific.
- Speak in a way that encourages dialogue.
- Be brief and to the point.
- Listen with respect.
- Listen for understanding.
- Be open to transformation.
- Stay in the circle. Respect for the circle calls upon people to stay in the circle while the circle works to find resolutions to the issues raised.

For more information on the Circle Process, please contact the JustPeace Center for Mediation and Conflict Transformation at http://justpeaceumc.org/.

A WORD TO THE COURSE PARTICIPANTS

(*Leader: Distribute prior to the first session.*)

Everyone participating in this advanced Lay Servant Ministries course is a recognized leader. Some participants will have many years of experience as leaders; others are just dipping their toes into the leadership pool. Some feel comfortable and confident as lay leaders; others feel unsure and hesitant. Some of you may already have strong preconceptions about what it means to be a leader; others may be confused or puzzled.

By the end of this course, you will know how to do these six things:

1. Expand your network of support as a lay servant
2. Deepen your understanding of the Social Principles as a "means of grace"
3. Identify and work through personal resistance to change
4. Discern how your congregation implements the Social Principles
5. Understand, form, and nurture new partnerships
6. Create a hospitable climate for teaching and practicing the Social Principles

This course uses the following approaches to learning:

Reading reveals basic information. We will look at what the Social Principles say and what they leave unsaid. We will practice reading the Social Principles analogically: In what ways do the Social Principles reflect the stories of your community, the church, and the world?

Dialogue connects new information to what we already know and practice. We will practice respectful dialogue as we learn about the Social Principles.

Journaling is an opportunity to reflect in or out of class on what we've discussed. Participants will need to bring their journals and pens or pencils to each class session.

Activities integrate new learning into our practice of lay ministry. We will practice several experiential exercises intended to take us into a deeper understanding of the Social Principles and their relevance for our lives and our congregations.

Please arrive on time and stay until each session is over. Come prepared to learn. Work toward adopting a nonjudgmental stance toward others, and seek to understand rather than convince others that their perspectives are wrong. Keep your eyes, ears, and hearts open, your imaginations keen, and your hopes high.

Since all participants are leaders, the group will ensure that everyone has equal time to share their ideas, directing participants to address their remarks to the group rather than to a particular individual. The group will agree to value the experiences and opinions of others even in moments of disagreement. The group will give permission for the teacher or facilitator to monitor and keep track of how the group is living up to this commitment.

Practice What You Learn: All meaningful learning involves changes in our behavior. As you read and talk with others in your class, consider how you can apply what you are learning. What opportunities exist to integrate new insights into how you participate in your local church's activities?

During this course, you will have opportunities to practice what you are learning through:

- group activities
- assignments
- the means of grace

Following this course, you will have opportunities to apply what you have learned through:

- assuming new leadership in your congregation, cluster, district, or conference
- building new concepts and strategies into your modeling, mentoring, teaching, and ministry

ALTERNATE WORSHIP PATTERNS

The following section contains alternate worship patterns you might wish to use for each session. You may substitute one or more of these for the opening and/or closing worship time as they appear in each session.

Session One

Opening Worship (10 Minutes). In his sermon titled "The Great Privilege of Those That Are Born of God," John Wesley said the following:

> I feel thee in all my ways: "Thou besettest me behind and before, and layest thy hand upon me." The Spirit or breath of God is immediately inspired, breathed into the new-born soul; and the same breath which comes from, returns to, God: As it is continually received by faith, so it is continually rendered back by love, by prayer, and praise, and thanksgiving; love and praise, and prayer being the breath of every soul which is truly born of God. And by this new kind of spiritual respiration, spiritual life is not only sustained, but increased day by day, together with spiritual strength, and motion, and sensation; all the senses of the soul being now awake, and capable of discerning spiritual good and evil."[15]

Ask for prayer concerns and then offer a prayer (such as "For Holiness of Heart" [*UMH*,no. 401]). Then read "God of the Sparrow, God of the Whale" (*UMH*, no. 122). Invite someone to read Ephesians 3:14-21 aloud.

Use a globe or world map, a potted plant, and a candle as centering symbols for worship.

Closing Prayer (5 Minutes). Close with either an extemporaneous prayer or one of the prayers listed below.

> Dear God, you have made us as co-creators of the earth;
> you have entrusted us with all resources of the world to care for and share.
> Help us always to be gentle with our planet.
> Help us not to pollute the atmosphere or waterways.
> Help us not to waste precious resources.
>
> Dear God, we know that the food we eat and drink is grown by people far away. Even though we will never meet them, help us to care for their needs as well as our own. Amen.
>
> —Christian Aid

> So if you want to understand the body of Christ, listen to the apostle telling the faithful, "You, though, are the body of Christ and its members" (1 Corinthians 12:27). So if it's you that are the body of Christ and its members it's the mystery meaning you that has been placed on the Lord's Table. What you receive is the mystery that means you. It is to what you are that you reply, Amen. . . . So be a member of the body of Christ, in order to make that "Amen" true.
>
> —Augustine, Sermon 272[16]

> Blessed be the Lord, the God of Israel. . . . Through His holy prophets He promised of old that He would save us from our enemies, from the hands of all who hate us. He promised to show mercy to our fathers, and to remember His holy Covenant.
>
> —Canticle of Zechariah[17]

> Glory to your mercy, glory to your power, glory to you! Without change, you are always completely in movement, completely outside creation and completely in every creature, you fill everything completely, you are completely outside of everything and above everything, you are not separated from the world, for you are in everything, but above everything.
>
> —Saint Symeon, *Hymns of Divine Love*[18]

Amazing grace! How sweet the sound that saved a wretch like me.
I once was lost, but now am found; was blind, but now I see.

—John Newton, "Amazing Grace"[19]

Session Two

Opening Worship (10 Minutes). Read or sing together "Woman in the Night" (*UMH*, no. 274). Ask the group for any prayer concerns. Invite the group to pray for the needs spoken by the group and pray aloud "For God's Gifts" (*UMH*, no. 489) or "The Servant Song" (*TFWS*, no. 2222).

Read Romans 3:14-21 aloud and invite the group to reflect on the meaning of Paul's words. Then ask the following questions:

- What do you hear in this scripture passage?
- How does it make you feel?
- How do you imagine the first Christian communities responded to Paul's words in this passage?

Closing Prayer (5 Minutes)

Eternal Spirit,
Earth-Maker, Pain-bearer, Life-giver,
Source of all that is and that shall be,
Father and Mother of us all,
Loving God, in whom is heaven:

The hallowing of your name echoes through the universe!
The way of your justice be followed by the peoples
    of the world!
Your heavenly will be done by all created beings!
Your commonwealth of peace and freedom
    sustain our hope and come on earth.

With the bread we need for today, feed us,
In the hurts we absorb from one another, forgive us.

In times of temptation and test, spare us.
From the grip of all that is evil, free us.

For you reign in the glory of the power that is love,
 now and forever. Amen.[20]

Session Three

Opening Worship (10 Minutes). Ask for prayer concerns from the class, and then pray "Prayer to the Holy Spirit" (*UMH*, no. 329).

Read these words from John Wesley's sermon titled "The Use of Money":

> We are . . . to gain all we can without hurting our neighbor. But this we may not, cannot do, if we love our neighbor as ourselves. We cannot, if we love everyone as ourselves, hurt anyone *in his substance*. We cannot devour the increase of his lands, and perhaps the lands and houses themselves, by gaming, by overgrown bills (whether on account of physic, or law, or anything else), or by requiring or taking such interest as even the laws of our country forbid. Hereby all pawn-brokering is excluded.[21]

Read 1 Corinthians 1:9-11 aloud. Invite responses to this passage in light of our Social Principles. Close worship by reading together "Where Shall My Wandering Soul Begin" (*UMH*, no. 342).

Closing Prayer (5 Minutes)

O God, whose will is justice for the poor and peace for the afflicted,
let your herald's voice pierce our hardened hearts and announce the dawn of your kingdom.
Before the Advent of the one who baptizes with the fire of the Holy Spirit,
let our complacency give way to conversion, oppression to justice,
and conflict to acceptance of one another in Christ.
We ask this through him whose coming is certain,
whose day draws near:
your son, our Lord Jesus Christ,
who lives and reigns with you and the Holy Spirit,
one God, forever and ever. Amen.[22]

Session Four

Opening Worship (10 Minutes). Ask for prayer concerns from the class. After praying with the group, sing "Our Earth We Now Lament to See" (*UMH*, no. 449). Then read Psalm 130 responsively (*UMH*, no. 848).

Consider discussing the following scriptures on peace as found in the Council of Bishops document *In Search of Security*. To live in safety is an unconditional promise of God (see Deut. 12:10; 33:12, 28). Israel lived in safety as long as its leaders followed God (see 1 Sam. 12:11 and 1 Kings 4:25).

Trust is equivalent to salvation and security in the biblical worldview. Safety does not begin with power to defend or preemptive strikes but with trust in God. "I will have pity on the house of Judah, and I will save them by the Lord their God; I will not save them by bow, or by sword, or by war, or by horses, or by horsemen" (Hos. 1:7). Consider the story of King Hezekiah as a model for alternative peace-building (see Isa. 36–39; 2 Kings 18–20).

Real security is a gift of God. Those who live safely and in peace and who do justice will live in security. The question with which we are faced in the twenty-first century is: When our own security or the security around us is threatened, should military intervention take place? There is no way to peace—peace is the way. Preemption understood as war is contrary to traditional moral norms because war is a last resort.

War has no built-in program to change things nor to rebuild what was destroyed in a new way. The real way to security is reconciliation—the transformative process of eliciting, coordinating, and strengthening the elements of community in both domestic and international societies. The stronger the community and its ethos, customs, and laws, the stronger the invisible and presupposed security to be free and to be vulnerable. The greater the invisible security of a people's common will and supportive social fabric, the less the need for visible, coercive, security forces.

Closing Prayer (5 Minutes). Pray the Prayer of Saint Francis aloud or silently.

Lord, make me an instrument of thy peace;
where there is hatred, let me sow love;
where there is injury, pardon;
where there is doubt, faith;
where there is despair, hope;

where there is darkness, light;
and where there is sadness, joy.

O Divine Master,
grant that I may not so much seek
to be consoled as to console;
to be understood, as to understand;
to be loved as to love;
for it is in giving that we receive,
it is in pardoning that we are pardoned,
and it is in dying that we are born to eternal life.[23]

Session Five

Opening Worship (10 Minutes). Ask for prayer concerns from the class and pray together "Concerning the Scriptures" (*UMH*, no. 602). Read or sing "Thy Word Is a Lamp" (*UMH*, no. 601). Invite one of the participants to read 1 Peter 1:22-25 aloud. Invite the class to think of how this passage relates to the Social Principles.

Closing Prayer (10 Minutes). Read aloud the 2008 Companion Litany to Our Social Creed from the *Social Principles* aloud.

NOTES

1. Ecclesiastes 3:1-8 (*The Message*).

2. Richard Wilcox, "Spain," in Maren C. Tirabassi, *Gifts of Many Cultures: Worship Resources for the Global Community* (Cleveland: United Church Press, 1995).

3. Global Ministries, "'The Character of a Methodist,' by John Wesley," accessed April 13, 2014, http://www.umcmission.org/Find-Resources/John-Wesley-Sermons/The-Wesleys-and-Their-Times/The-Character-of-a-Methodist.

4. "Night Prayer," in *A New Zealand Prayer Book*, http://anglicanprayerbook.org.nz/167.html.

5. "A Covenant Prayer in the Wesleyan Tradition" (*UMH*, 607).

6. Gilbert Hay, *The Father Gilbert Prayer Book*, 1st ed. (Silver Spring, MD: Trinity Missions, 1965).

7. Geoffrey Duncan, ed., *Harvest for the World* (Norwich: Canterbury Press, 2002), 119.

8. Bruce S. Feiler, *Walking the Bible: A Journey by Land Through the Five Books of Moses* (New York: HarperCollins, 2002).

9. Mara Vanderslice and Eric Sapp, "Policy Maker's Guide to Poverty, Social Justice, and the Prophetic Voice in the Bible—Oregon PeaceWorks," accessed April 13, 2014, http://oregonpeaceworks.org/item/30-policy-maker-s-guide-to-poverty-social-justice-and-the-prophetic-voice-in-the-bible.

10. *Doctrines and Discipline of the Methodist Episcopal Church—1928* (Methodist Book Concern, 1928).

11. See UNICEF, "Narrowing the Gaps to Meet the Goals Study and Progress for Children: Achieving the MDGs with Equity Key Facts," www.unicef.org/ FINAL_MDGs_with_Equity_Key_Facts; and United Nations, "Fact Sheet: Goal 8: Develop a global partnership for development," http://www.un.org/millenniumgoals/pdf/Goal_8_fs.pdf.

12. This account is from a "Methodist Church Tract," one of many widely distributed by our church in 1906.

13. Reinhold Niebuhr, *The Essential Reinhold Niebuhr: Selected Essays and Addresses*, ed. Robert McAfee Brown (New Haven, CT: Yale University Press, 1986), xii.

14. Global Ministries, John Wesley, Sermon 39, "Catholic Spirit," accessed April 14, 2014, http://www.umcmission.org/Find-Resources/John-Wesley-Sermons/Sermon-39-Catholic-Spirit.

15. Global Ministries, John Wesley, Sermon 19, "The Great Privilege of Those That Are Born of God," accessed April 14, 2014, http://www.umcmission.org/Find-Resources/John-Wesley -Sermons/Sermon-19-The-Great-Privilege-of-Those-that-Are-Born-of-God.

16. "Augustine Sermon 272 on The Eucharist," accessed April 14, 2014, http://www.early churchtexts.com/public/augustine_sermon_272_eucharist.htm.

17. "Canticle of Zechariah—Prayers—Catholic Online," accessed April 14, 2014, http:// www.catholic.org/prayers/prayer.php?p=542.

18. "A Neglected Masterpiece of the Christian Mystical Tradition," accessed April 14, 2014, http://www.sgtt.org/Writings/Patristics/StSymeonHymns.html.

19. John Newton, "Amazing Grace" (*UMH*, no. 378).

20. "The Lord's Prayer," in *A New Zealand Prayer Book*, http://anglicanprayerbook.org.nz /167.html.

21. Global Ministries, John Wesley, Sermon 50, "The Use of Money," http://www.umcmission .org/Find-Resources/John-Wesley-Sermons/Sermon-50-The-Use-of-Money.

22. Salisbury Presbyterian Church, "Advent Word for Day 13—Justice," http://www.the salisburychurch.org/welcome/blog/advent-day-13-justice.

23. "The Prayer of Saint Francis" (*UMH*, no. 481).

CPSIA information can be obtained at www.ICGtesting.com
Printed in the USA
LVOW03s2346280115

424779LV00002B/9/P